A Guide for Using

Little House in the Big Woods

in the Classroom

Based on the novel written by
Laura Ingalls Wilder

This guide written by Laurie Swinwood

Teacher Created Resources, Inc.
6421 Industry Way
Westminster, CA 92683
www.teachercreated.com
ISBN: 978-1-55734-522-6
©*1994 Teacher Created Resources, Inc.*
Reprinted, 2012
Made in U.S.A.

Illustrated by
Agi Palinay

Cover Art by
Nancee McClure

Table of Contents

Introduction

A good book can touch our lives like a good friend. Within its pages are words and characters that can inspire us to achieve our highest ideals. We can turn to it for companionship, recreation, comfort, and guidance. It can also give us a cherished story to hold in our hearts forever.

In *Literature Units,* great care has been taken to select books that are sure to become good friends!

Teachers who use this literature unit will find the following features to supplement their own valuable ideas.

- Sample Lesson Plans

- Pre-reading Activities

- Biographical Sketch and Picture of the Author

- Book Summary

- Vocabulary Lists and Suggested Vocabulary Activity Ideas

- Chapters grouped for study with the sections including:

    — *quizzes*

    — *hands-on projects*

    — *cooperative learning activities*

    — *cross-curriculum connections*

    — *extensions into the reader's life*

- Post-reading Activities

- Book Report Ideas

- Research Ideas

- Culminating Activities

- Three Different Options for Unit Tests

- Bibliography

- Answer Key

We are confident that this unit will be a valuable addition to your planning, and we hope that as you use our ideas, your students will increase the circle of "friends" they have in books!

Sample Lesson Plan

Each of the lessons below can take from one to several days to complete.

Lesson 1
- Introduce and complete some or all of the pre-reading activities. (page 5)
- Read "About the Author" with your students. (page 6)
- Introduce the vocabulary list for Section 1. (page 8)

Lesson 2
- Read chapters 1 and 2. As you read, place the vocabulary words in the context of the story and discuss their meanings.
- Choose a vocabulary activity. (page 9)
- Make paper dolls. (page 11)
- Research panthers. (page 12)
- Label a map of Wisconsin. (page 13)
- Describe Laura's home and your home. (page 14)
- Administer the Section 1 quiz. (page 10)
- Introduce the vocabulary list for Section 2. (page 8)

Lesson 3
- Read chapters 3–5. Place the vocabulary words in context and discuss their meanings.
- Choose a vocabulary activity. (page 9)
- Make an apple pomander ball. (page 16)
- Create a book in the shape of a house. (page 17)
- Tell a story from an owl's point of view. (page 18)
- Compare special holidays. (page 19)
- Administer the Section 2 quiz. (page 15)
- Introduce the vocabulary list for Section 3. (page 8)

Lesson 4
- Read chapters 6–8. Place the vocabulary words in context and discuss their meanings.
- Choose a vocabulary activity. (page 9)
- Make a lantern. (page 21)
- Make maple sugar candy. (page 22)
- Learn how to square dance. (page 23)

- Complete a family tree. (page 24)
- Administer the Section 3 quiz. (page 20)
- Introduce the vocabulary list for Section 4. (page 8)

Lesson 5
- Read chapters 9–10. Place the vocabulary words in context and discuss their meanings.
- Choose a vocabulary activity. (page 9)
- Make a patchwork quilt from construction paper. (page 26)
- Build your own town. (page 27)
- Learn about honey bees. (page 28)
- Write a journal entry. (page 29)
- Administer the Section 4 quiz. (page 25)
- Introduce the vocabulary list for Section 5. (page 8)

Lesson 6
- Read chapters 11–13. Place the vocabulary words in context and discuss their meanings.
- Choose a vocabulary activity. (page 9)
- Make stewed pumpkin. (page 31)
- Write a pioneer cookbook. (page 32)
- Compare and contrast "The Boy Who Cried Wolf" with a boy's experience in the story. (page 33)
- Make an autograph book. (page 34)
- Administer the Section 5 quiz. (page 30)

Lesson 7
- Discuss any questions your students may have about the story. (page 35)
- Assign book reports and research projects. (pages 36 and 37)
- Begin work on culminating activities. (pages 38, 39, and 40)

Lesson 8
- Administer unit tests 1,2, and/or 3. (pages 41, 42, and 43)
- Discuss the test answers and possibilities.
- Discuss the students' enjoyment of the book.
- Provide a list of related reading for your students. (page 44)

Before the Book

Literature is always more meaningful when the reader is given a solid background before reading. Children need to have a feel for the time period, the characters, and the author of the book. The following activities may work well with your class.

1. Discuss with students any other books they have read by Laura Ingalls Wilder.

2. Set up a cozy reading corner in your classroom. Display Laura Ingalls Wilder's books in that corner.

3. Predict what the story might be about by hearing the title and looking at the cover illustration or by previewing the illustrations in the book.

4. Answer these questions.

   • Are you interested in . . .
      stories about the hardships of pioneer life?
      stories about family life?
      stories that involve danger from wild animals?

   • Would you ever . . .
      want to live where there were no houses, people, or roads?
      be afraid of a screech owl?
      slap a wild bear on the shoulder?

5. Create an Ingalls Bulletin Board. Have students draw pictures of Laura and her family. They may want to draw pictures of the setting as well to create a "Little House in the Big Woods" scene.

6. Using the *Laura Ingalls Wilder Songbook* by Eugenia Garson, learn a few of the songs Laura heard her father sing, such as "Old Dan Tucker," "Oh! Susanna," and "Old Grimes."

7. Use an atlas to locate a map that shows Wisconsin, the setting of the story.

8. Do research to learn about the post-Civil War years.

9. Borrow trunks of artifacts from that time period from your local museum. Share with your students. (If this is not possible, make your own trunk and have students make models of artifacts.)

10. Make time each day to read aloud to your class from one of the books by Laura Ingalls Wilder.

About the Author

Laura Elizabeth Ingalls was born on February 7, 1867, in the Big Woods of Pepin, Wisconsin. Her parents were Charles and Caroline Ingalls. Laura was their second child.

In 1870 Laura's father packed up the family and their belongings in a covered wagon. They settled in Montgomery County, Kansas, which was called Indian Territory at that time. After living on the Kansas prairie, the Ingalls family moved back to Wisconsin in 1871, and then to Plum Creek in Minnesota in 1874. They lived there for several years, although one year was spent as caretakers for a hotel in Burr Oak, Iowa. In 1879, they moved to the new town of DeSmet near Silver Lake in the Dakota Territory. This area is now in the state of South Dakota.

In 1882, when Laura was 15, she became a teacher. The school in which she taught was an abandoned claim shanty. It was located twelve miles from De Smet. When Laura was 18, she married Almanzo Wilder, who was 28. In 1886, they had a daughter, Rose. Two years later, they had a son who died in infancy. When Rose was a young child, Laura and Almanzo moved to Spring Valley, Minnesota, for one year to stay with Almanzo's parents, and they moved to the piney woods of Florida. After a short while, they returned to De Smet. Finally, in 1894, they moved for the last time to Rocky Ridge Farm in Mansfield, Missouri.

In 1911 Laura started writing articles about farming. She was 44 when she became a household editor and her first article was published in the *Missouri Ruralist*. Her daughter, Rose, was a successful journalist. She encouraged her mother to write an autobiography.

Laura wrote about her childhood in a story entitled "Pioneer Girl." The story began when she was a little girl living in the Big Woods of Pepin, Wisconsin, and ended when she got married. However, Laura was not able to find anyone who would publish it. As a result, she decided to rewrite it as a series of children's books telling about her experiences as a pioneer child. She called the first book *Little House in the Big Woods*. In 1932, when Laura was sixty-five years old, the book was published by Harper and Brothers.

To Laura's surprise, *Little House in the Big Woods* was an enormous success, not only with children but with literary critics as well. Over the next eleven years, she wrote an entire series of books which includes *Farmer Boy* (1933), *Little House on the Prairie* (1935), *On the Banks of Plum Creek* (1937), *By the Shores of Silver Lake* (1939), *The Long Winter* (1940), *Little Town on the Prairie* (1941), and *These Happy Golden Years* (1943). Laura won a variety of honors and awards for these books. She was the first person to receive an award from the Children's Library Association for her lasting contribution to children's literature, and the Laura Ingalls Wilder award was named in her honor.

Laura died on February 10, 1957, at the age of 90. Her memories have provided readers with an insight into the sacrifices and hardships of pioneer life. Laura's books have remained popular with readers of all ages. They have been translated into many foreign languages. Her books were also the basis for a popular television series called "Little House on the Prairie."

Little House in the Big Woods
by Laura Ingalls Wilder

(Harper & Row, 1932)
(Also available in Canada, UK & AUS from HarperChild Bks.)

The story begins when Laura Ingalls was a little girl living in a log cabin in the Big Woods of Wisconsin. She lived with her mother and father, whom she called Ma and Pa, an older sister named Mary, and a baby sister named Carrie. Mary was always a very good girl and did exactly what she was told. She loved to cook, sew, and help around the house. In contrast, Laura was extremely bored by sewing. She would rather have been outside climbing trees than inside working.

The Ingalls cabin was surrounded by woods. They did not have any neighbors except for the wild animals that shared the woods with them. Life in the cabin was comfortable but not without its dangers from the wild animals. For example, one night Ma and Laura went to milk their cow. When they got to the pen, the gate was being blocked by an animal they thought was their cow. Ma slapped the animal on the shoulder to move it out of the way. Suddenly, Ma and Laura realized that it was a bear in the pen and not their cow.

The story describes in detail what life was like for the Ingalls family. Everyone worked hard doing chores during the day. They had to work together to provide for all of their needs. They got milk from their cow, churned their own butter, and made their own cheese. They grew their own crops and raised animals for meat. Pa also got meat for the family by hunting wild animals such as deer and bear. Then in the evening, the family was entertained by Pa's fiddle playing and storytelling. One tale Pa related to the family was about an experience he had as a young boy when he had not listened to his father. He explained that he was rounding up the cows from the woods when he began to play. As it grew dark, he frantically called out the names of the cows but could not find them. Suddenly, he heard a voice asking, "Who?" It scared him so badly he ran all the way home. When he arrived, he found that the cows were already there and that the voice he had heard was nothing more than a screech owl.

Vocabulary Lists

The vocabulary words which are listed below correspond to each section of *Little House in the Big Woods*, as outlined in the table of contents. Ideas for vocabulary activities are found on page 9 of this book.

Section 1 (Chapters 1–2)

fierce	trundle bed	bladder	johnnycake	churn
hickory	brindle bulldog	headcheese	pantry	panther
muskrats	venison	spareribs	thimble	buttermilk
mink	butcher	spices	kerosene	woodbox

Section 2 (Chapters 3–5)

bullet-mold	cowhorn	curlicues	thrashing	hot griddle
hearth	gunpowder	mufflers	gaiters	flatirons
gunstock	crescent moons	ravines	buffalo robes	catechism
jackknife	ramrod	stout switch	savage	washtub

Section 3 (Chapters 6–8)

quivered	scalp	flannel	hasty pudding	cameo
lantern	trough	maple sugar	petticoats	calico
winter-starved	sap	sugar snow	corset	basque
basswood	latchstring	delaine	pattypan	flounce

Section 4 (Chapters 9–10)

muzzle	fawn	storekeeper	galluses	curdcheese
wisp	curried	jumper	greedy	hoop
unselfish	stockings	wagonbox	rennet	whey
slender	sunbonnets	sulked	heifers	honeycomb

Section 5 (Chapters 11–13)

cradles	shock	eight-horsepower	herbs	threshing machine
grain	whetstone	yellow jacket	horrified	yearling
stalk	rind	separator	monstrously	deerlick
hulls	braid	progress	threshers	fiddle

8

Vocabulary Activity Ideas

Little House in the Big Woods is rich with vocabulary from the pioneer era. The ideas below will help your students learn and retain that vocabulary.

- Divide the class into two teams. Ask both teams to *Locate a Vocabulary Word* in a section of the book. A team earns a point if they locate the word first. If that team can give the correct definition for the word, they earn another point. Continue playing with other vocabulary words. A team wins when they have the greatest number of points at the end of a period of time that you specify.

- Have a *Vocabulary Bee.* This is similar to a Spelling Bee. The students must be able to spell the word and define it, as well.

- Have students make a *Part of Speech Categories Chart* with headings such as Noun, Verb, Adjective, and Adverb. Then have them list each vocabulary word under the appropriate heading.

- Make a *Pioneer Dictionary,* complete with definitions and sentences.

- Prepare a spinner to play *Spin-a-Word* by drawing lines to divide it into four equal parts. Mark each part with one of the following point values: 10 points, 20 points, 30 points, 40 points. Divide the class into two teams. Play the game by having each student spin the spinner and define a vocabulary word that you provide. A correct answer is worth the point value shown on the spinner. Then the spinner goes to the other team. A wrong answer means the spinner goes to the other team without any points being scored. The team with the highest total score at the end of a period of time that you designate is the winner.

- Have students create a *Wordsearch* or a *Crossword Puzzle* to exchange with a partner. Then have them check each other's paper.

- Have students use these words as their weekly *Spelling List.*

- Group your students into teams to play a *Word Game.* Give each student a slate, a piece of chalk and a dictionary. Give the whole class one of the words to define, using the dictionary. Team members may help one another. Members must write the definitions on their slates. If everyone on the team has the correct answer, the team earns a point. (The teacher keeps score on the blackboard.) The team with the most points at the end of a given period of time is the winning team. This game may be varied. The teacher might give the meaning and the team members give the word, or the team might be requested to give the word and the correct part of speech, or they might be asked to write the word in a sentence.

- Have students create *Alphables* by listing the words in alphabetical order and dividing them into syllables.

Quiz Time!

1. On the back of this paper, write a one-paragraph summary of the major events in Chapters 1 and 2. Then complete the rest of the questions on this page.

2. Who is the author of *Little House in the Big Woods*? _____

    _____

3. What is the setting of the story? _____

    _____

4. What part of the pig did Laura and Mary like best? Explain why. _____

    _____

5. What is a trundle bed? _____

    _____

6. What kind of doll was Laura's doll, Susan? _____

    _____

7. Why did Pa bring both a bear and a pig home? _____

    _____

8. On the back of this paper, tell what happened in Pa's story, "The Story of Grandpa and the Panther."

9. Describe the game called "Mad Dog." Why do you think Laura and Mary enjoyed playing it?

    _____

    _____

    _____

    _____

10. Would you like to live like Laura did? Explain why or why not.

    _____

    _____

    _____

Make Paper Dolls

At the end of the day, Ma often cut paper dolls for Laura and Mary. She cut the bodies from stiff white paper and the clothes and ribbons from brightly colored paper. Use the outline of the boy and girl shown below to create your own paper dolls.

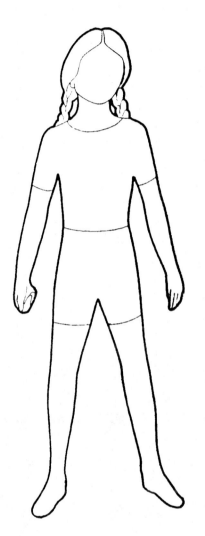
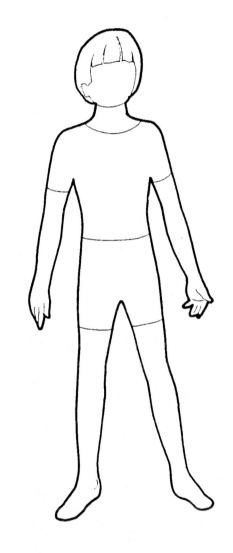

Materials:

- stiff white paper • scissors • colored paper • colored pencils

Directions:

Trace the bodies of the boy and girl onto stiff white paper. Then cut them out. Use colored pencils to draw their faces. Design their clothes and shoes or boots. Draw and cut these out of the colored paper. Be sure to cut small tabs of paper along the edges so that the clothing may be attached to the dolls by folding the tabs. Here is an example of how to make the tabs.

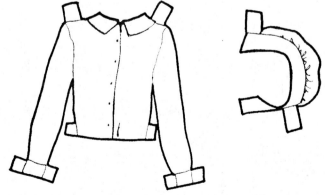

Panther Research

An outline is a good way to organize information. The title of an outline tells what the subject is. Use Roman numerals, such as I., II., and III. . . . to tell the main ideas. Use capital letters, (A., B., and C. . . . to tell the details about each main idea. Put a period after each Roman numeral and capital letter. Use words and phrases rather than sentences to write each main idea and detail. Capitalize only the first word for each entry on the outline.

Here is an example:

Black Bears

  I. Description (what they look like)
     A. Head — broad, extended jaw, pointed muzzle, small eyes
     B. Paws — flat-footed, powerful claws
     C. Hair — shaggy, black
     D. Height and weight— 3–10' (1–3 m); 60–1,720 lbs (27–780 kg)

 II. Habitat (where they live)
     A. North America
     B. Northern temperate regions

III. Foods
     A. Omnivores—eat meat and vegetables
     B. Food sources—ants, honey, bees, seeds, roots, berries, nuts, insect larvae, rodents, fish, deer, pigs, lambs

In Chapter 2, Pa tells Laura and Mary a story about his father being chased by a panther. Work with three or four other students to research panthers. Use the outline below to organize your information. Then draw an illustration of a panther on the back of your outline.

Panthers

  I. Description
     A. _____
     B. _____
     C. _____
     D. _____

 II. Habitat
     A. _____
     B. _____

III. Foods
     A. _____
     B. _____

A Map of Wisconsin

The Ingalls lived in the state of Wisconsin. Locate a map of Wisconsin in an atlas, encyclopedia, or other reference book. On the map below, locate the following places and label them on the map. The first one is done for you. After you have finished labeling your map, you may wish to color it.

Lake Superior	Lake Michigan	Green Bay
Lake Pepin	Mississippi River	Saint Croix River
Chippewa River	Menominee River	Madison
		Pepin

Lake Superior

Show a state capital symbol for Madison. _____

Show a city/town symbol for Pepin. _____

Show a compass rose with the cardinal directions labeled (N, S, E, W). _____

Homes: Today and Yesterday

Laura's home was very different from most of the homes people live in today. Write a description of Laura's home inside the log cabin shown below. Then write a description of your house or apartment inside the modern house shown below.

Quiz Time!

1. On the back of this paper, write a one-paragraph summary of the major events in chapters 3, 4, and 5 in this section. Then complete the rest of the questions on this page.

2. What was the "voice in the woods" that Pa had heard when he was a young boy?

   _____

3. How did Laura and Mary make the molasses candy?

   _____

   _____

4. Who came to visit Laura's family at Christmas?

   _____

5. What did Laura, Mary, and their cousins do all morning in the snow?

   _____

6. Why did Aunt Eliza's dog, Prince, act so strangely when she wanted to go down to the spring?

   _____

   _____

7. What gifts did Laura receive for Christmas?

   _____

8. What was every Sunday like for Laura and Mary?

   _____

   _____

   _____

9. On the back of this paper, retell "The Story of Grandpa's Sled and the Pig." Draw an illustration to go with the story.

10. What gifts did Laura receive for her birthday?

    _____

    _____

Apple Pomander Ball

You can make an apple pomander ball to help your kitchen smell as sweet as Laura's.

Materials:

- whole cloves
- an apple
- cinnamon
- a plastic bag (large enough for the apple)
- ribbon or wide yarn

Directions:

1. Hold the round part of the clove and stick the stem into the apple.

2. Continue sticking cloves into the apple until it is completely covered by the cloves.

3. Pour some cinnamon into the plastic bag. Then put the apple in the bag. Close the bag and shake it.

4. After removing the apple from the bag, tie two pieces of ribbon or yarn around the apple so that they criss-cross at the bottom and knot at the top. Then tie a third piece of ribbon or yarn to the top of the apple so that you can hang it in your kitchen.

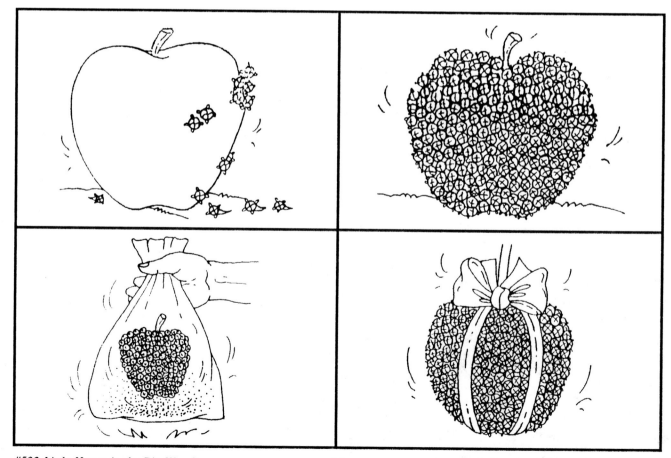

Create a "House" Book

Work with two or three other students to change ordinary drawing paper into a log cabin in this folding activity. Then write a story about your favorite part in this section of the book. Your story is shown when the doors of your log cabin are opened.

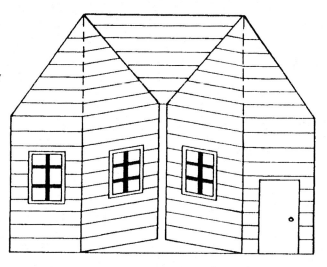

Materials:

- drawing paper or construction paper
- scissors
- crayons, colored pencils, or markers
- pencils
- writing paper
- glue or paste

Directions:

1. Fold a sheet of drawing or construction paper in half lengthwise.

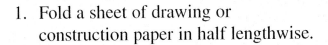

2. Open the paper and fold along the width.

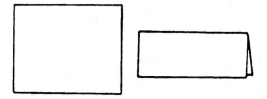

3. Fold each side into center.

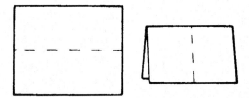

4. Unfold the sides and down the top corners to form triangles.

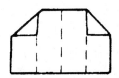

5. Unfold both triangles and push them inward.

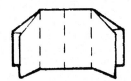

6. Fold the top layer inward toward the center to form door flaps. Work together to write a story that retells your favorite part of Chapters 3, 4, and 5. Be sure to use writing paper that is cut so it will fit in the space behind the doors when they are opened. After completing the story, glue it to the space behind the doors. Display your log cabin on a table so other students can read your story.

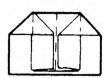

Owl's Story

Follow the directions shown below to make an owl puppet. Write a story on a separate piece of paper in which your owl tells its side of "The Story of Pa and the Voice in the Woods." You may wish to give the story a new title since your owl is telling it. Then have your owl puppet tell its story to your class.

Materials:

- a brown paper bag that will fit over your hand
- scissors
- glue or paste
- markers, crayons, or colored pencils
- construction paper

Directions:

1. Place the bag so that it is flat on the table. The bottom of the bag should be at the top and facing toward the table.
   (Look at the illustration as you follow Steps 2 through 5.)

2. To make the eyes, use yellow construction paper to cut two large yellow circles. Use black crayons, markers, or pencils to make a black circle in the center of each yellow circle. Draw short lines around each black circle. Then glue the eyes in place on the bag.

3. Use construction paper to cut a beak and the feathers that go above the eyes. Glue the beak and feathers in place on the bag.

4. Cut long strips of construction paper to make the body feathers. Then cut small slits all along one side of each strip to make fringe. Start at the bottom of the bag and glue on each strip of fringe.

5. Allow the glue to dry. Then place the bag on your hand.

Special Holidays: Past and Present

Christmas was a special holiday for Laura's family. Laura's Christmas was very different from most children's special holidays today. Illustrate Laura's Christmas, as described in Chapter 4, in the picture frame labeled Laura's Christmas. Then illustrate a holiday that is important to you in the picture frame labeled My Important Holiday.

Laura's Christmas

My Important Holiday

On the back of this paper, write a comparison of the two holidays you have illustrated. Tell how they are alike and how they are different. Then tell which holiday you like best and explain why.

Quiz Time!

1. On the back of this paper, write a one-paragraph summary of the major events in chapters 6,7, and 8 in this section. Then complete the rest of the questions on this page.

2. What happened when Ma and Laura went outside in the dark to feed Sukey?

   _____

3. What did Pa bring from town for Laura and Mary?

   _____

4. When Pa headed home after selling his furs, he thought that he had met a bear in the woods. What was it really?

   _____

5. What is *sugar snow*?

   _____

6. What does Grandpa make from the sap of his maple trees?

   _____

7. How did Pa and Grandpa carry the buckets of hot maple syrup?

   _____

8. Uncle George is quite a colorful character. Write a descriptive paragraph on the back of this paper about him.

9. At Grandpa's, Laura saw her cousin, Laura. What did the two girls argue about?

   _____

10. Describe the dance at Grandpa's. What was your favorite part?

    _____

    _____

    _____

Make a Lantern

Laura . . . carried the lantern very carefully. Its sides were of tin, with places cut in them for the candle-light to shine through. When Laura walked behind Ma the little bits of candlelight from the lantern leaped all around her on the snow.

In this activity, you can make a lantern like the one Laura used. Be very careful when working with the tin can since the sharp edges on the top and from inside the nail holes can hurt you.

Materials:

- different size nails
- hammer
- newspapers or towels
- sand
- flashlight shorter than the can
- a clean tin can, with the paper wrapper and glue removed, and with the bottom left on
- tin snips
- coat hanger
- a black crayon
- wide duct tape or masking tape

Directions:

1. Use a crayon to draw a picture on the can.

2. Fill the can with sand. Put the can on a stack of newspapers or an old towel. This will stop the can from rolling and protect the table on which you are working.

3. Work on only one part of the can at a time. Use the nails to make different sized holes. Hammer the nails into the can along the lines of the picture you have drawn. When you are finished making holes, empty the sand from the can.

4. Have an adult use tin snips to cut a coat hanger so it can be used as a handle. Attach the handle through two holes you have made in the can.

5. Roll a piece of wide tape and place it at the bottom of the can. Turn on the flashlight and stick it on the tape in the can. Turn off the classroom lights.

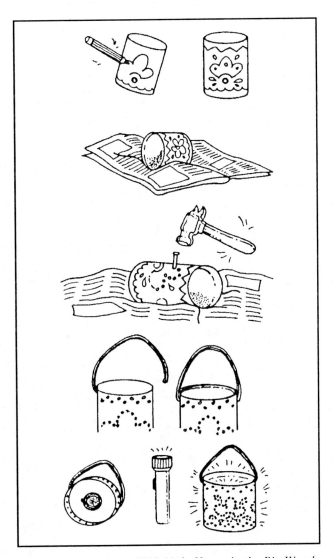

Maple Sugar Candy

Work with three or four other students to make your own maple sugar candy by following the recipe shown below. Be sure to work under the direction of an adult and follow kitchen safety rules.

Materials:

- hot plate
- 3-quart (2.85 L) pot
- ½ gallon (1.9 L) of maple syrup
- butter
- candy molds
- hot mitts

Directions:

1. Butter the candy molds.

2. Pour 2 cups (500 mL) of maple syrup into the pot.

3. Carefully place the pot on the hot plate.

4. Bring the syrup to a slow boil, stirring constantly.

5. As syrup begins to turn grainy, pour it into the buttered candy molds.

6. Allow the syrup to set for half an hour or until hard. Then pop the candies out of the molds.

Square Dancing

Then Pa took his fiddle out of its box and began to play, and all the couples stood in squares on the floor, and began to dance when Pa called the figures. 'Grand right and left' Pa called out.

Follow the directions below to do the same square dance that Pa was calling.

Directions:

1. Everyone has a partner. Four partners stand in a square formation, making a group of eight.

2. Each person faces a partner and lightly shakes the partner's right hand.

3. Partners on the right weave around the circle to the left.

4. Partners on the left weave around the circle to the right.

5. Each time the dancers pass a new person, they shake that person's hand, alternating from left to right hand each time.

6. The dancers pass right shoulders, then left shoulders, until the partners meet again.

7. When the partners meet, they join arms and twirl around in place, completing a full circle.

Note to the Teacher: You may wish to borrow a square dancing record from the physical education department or your library. Another good resource is Betty Casey's book, *The Complete Book of Square Dancing* (Doubleday, 1976).

Family Trees

Laura's family tree is listed below. With the help of your parents and grandparents, fill in the second tree with members of your own family.

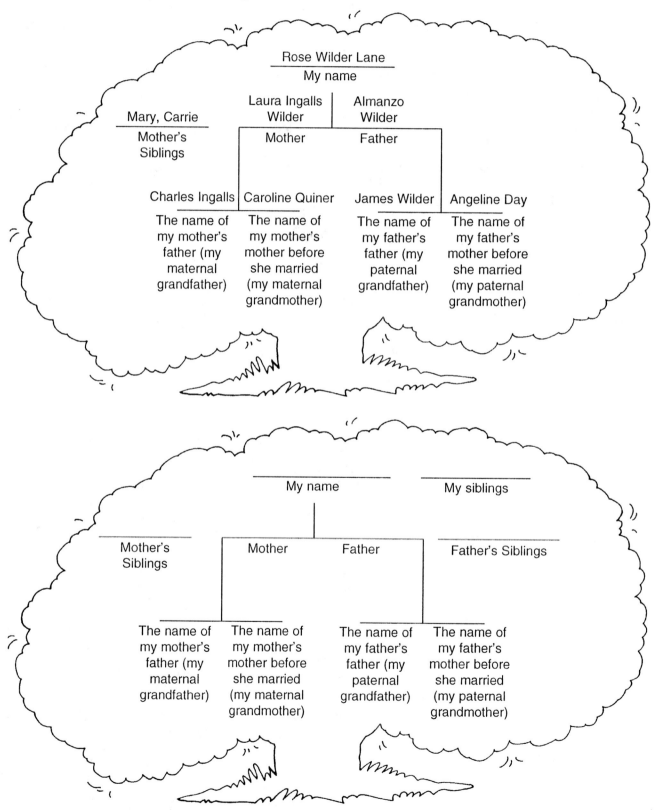

Quiz Time!

1. On the back of this paper, write a one-paragraph summary of the major events in chapters 9 and 10 in this section. Then complete the rest of the questions on this page.

2. Describe Laura's and Mary's playhouses.

   _____

3. Pa saw a doe and her fawn. Why didn't he shoot the doe?

   _____

4. What was the town of Pepin like?

   _____

5. What did the storekeeper give to Mary and Laura?

   _____

6. What happened to all the pretty pebbles that Laura collected at Lake Pepin?

   _____

7. Why did Laura like playing with Clarence better than playing with Eva?

   _____

8. Aunt Lotty said that she liked "...both kinds best," when asked which she liked, brown or golden hair the best. Why did this make Laura happy?

   _____

9. Why did Pa spank Laura?

   _____

10. How did Pa get honey away from a bear and the bees?

   _____

Patchwork Quilt

Quilting was a very popular craft among pioneer women in the 1800's. The quilts were made from three layers of fabric that were sewn together. The top of a quilt was often decorated using small pieces of colorful fabric to form a geometric design or a floral pattern. Laura and Mary's first quilts were nine-patch quilts. She and Mary sewed each piece carefully by hand.

In this activity, you will make your own patchwork quilt.

Materials:

- two sheets of butcher paper or other sturdy paper, each sheet: 2' x 2' (60 cm x 60 cm)
- 16 construction paper squares, each square: 6" x 6" (15 cm x 15 cm)
- colorful fabric scraps or pieces of construction paper
- glue

Directions:

1. Use the space below to plan what your quilt design will look like.

2. Glue the two sheets of butcher paper together. This will make the back of your quilt and the middle layer, which is called the interlining. Allow the glue to dry.

3. Decorate each construction paper square using colorful fabric scraps or pieces of construction paper. Allow the glue on the squares to dry.

4. Lay your squares on the interlining according to your design shown above. Then glue them down. Allow the glue to dry.

5. Display your patchwork quilt on a wall or bulletin board.

Build Your Own Town

When the Ingalls family was close to the town of Pepin, Pa stopped the wagon. Laura stood up on the board, and Pa held her safely by the arm so she could see the town. When she saw it she could hardly breathe. She knew how Yankee Doodle felt when he could not see the town because there were so many houses. Make a model of the town using Laura's description in Chapter 9, "Going to Town."

Materials:

- large box for the store
- gray posterboard
- sand
- several smaller boxes for houses
- large piece of blue posterboard for Lake Pepin
- tempera paints
- paintbrushes
- fabric scraps
- glue
- scissors
- piece of heavy cardboard or plywood, 3' x 3' (0.9 m x 0.9 m)

Directions:

1. Paint the large box gray to be the store. Let the paint dry. On the front of the store, paint a door and a window on each side of the door. Let the paint dry.

2. Use posterboard to make a platform and stairs for the store. Glue the platform and stairs onto the gray box.

3. Paint the smaller boxes yellow or gray like the houses. Let the paint dry. Paint doors and windows on the houses. Let the paint dry.

4. Use posterboard to make chimneys for the houses. Glue the chimneys to the houses.

5. Open the back end of each box to make the inside of the store and the houses.

6. Use fabric scraps to create curtains, the bolts of fabric for the store, the laundry that was spread out to dry on the bushes and stumps, bedcovers for the beds, as well as other things you can think of.

7. You may want to create paper dolls for Ma, Pa, Laura, Mary, Baby Carrie, the storekeeper, and the children at play and place them in the town.

8. Cut a large piece of blue posterboard to make Lake Pepin. Glue the lake onto the heavy cardboard or plywood.

9. Glue down the store at the edge of the lake. Leave an open area, then glue down the houses. Place sand around the base of the store and the houses.

Honey Bees

In the story Pa brought honey home from a bee tree that he had found. Work with a partner to learn more about honey bees. Use encyclopedias and other reference books to find the answers to the questions on this page.

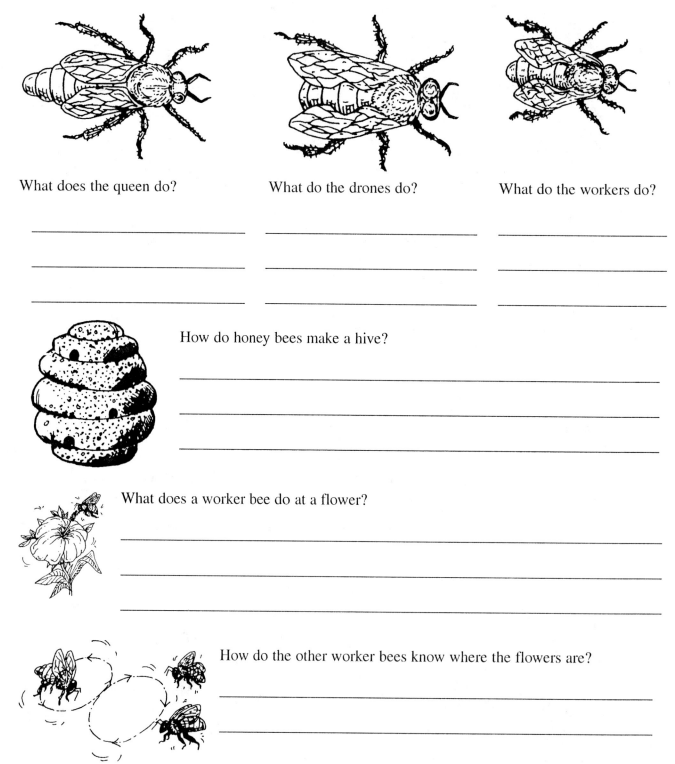

What does the queen do?

_____

_____

_____

What do the drones do?

_____

_____

_____

What do the workers do?

_____

_____

_____

How do honey bees make a hive?

_____

_____

_____

What does a worker bee do at a flower?

_____

_____

_____

How do the other worker bees know where the flowers are?

_____

_____

_____

Journal Entry

A journal is like a diary. It is a book in which you write about things that happen to you. In a journal entry you can tell what you think or how you feel about the things that happen. Pretend that you are Laura and write a journal entry. Tell about one of the things that happens to Laura in this section of the book.

Here are some ideas of things you can write about in your journal entry.

1. Laura seeing the town of Pepin for the first time
2. Laura at the store in Pepin
3. Laura's pocket tearing from all the heavy pebbles
4. Aunt Lotty's visit
5. Laura slapping Mary in the face

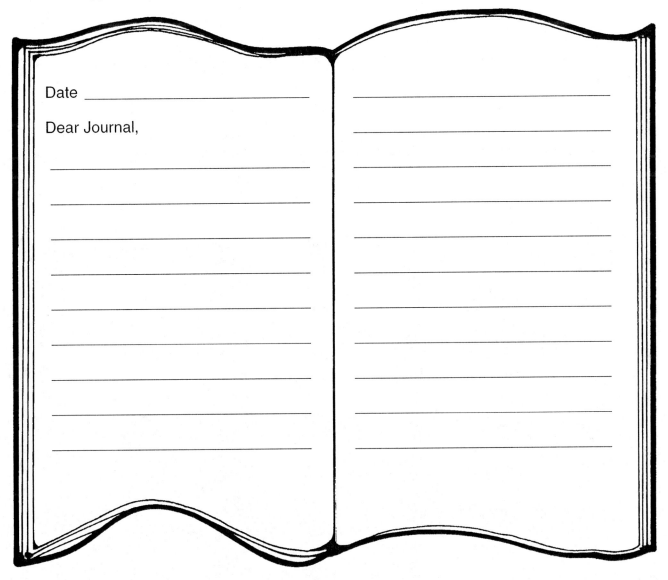

Date _____

Dear Journal,

Now share your journal entry with the class.

Quiz Time!

1. On the back of this paper, write a one-paragraph summary of the major events in chapters 11, 12, and 13 in this section. Then complete the rest of the questions on this page.

2. Pa used a cradle to harvest the oats. What is a cradle?

   _____

3. Why was it so important for Pa and Uncle Henry to put the stalks of cut grain safely in the shock before dark?

   _____

4. Write a descriptive paragraph about Cousin Charley.

   _____

5. How did Ma and Aunt Polly treat Charley's yellow jacket stings?

   _____

6. Pa said that Cousin Charley was a liar. Laura didn't understand how Charley could tell a lie without saying anything. Why do you think Pa said Charley lied?

   _____

7. What did Ma make from straw?

   _____

8. For what was the "wonderful machine" used?

   _____

9. What does it mean when a machine has "eight horsepower?"

   _____

10. At the end of the book, Laura said, "It can never be a long time ago." What do you think Laura meant by that?

    _____

    _____

Stewed Pumpkin

In this activity, you will learn to make stewed pumpkin like Laura helped Ma make. Be sure to work under the direction of an adult and follow kitchen safety rules.

Materials:

- large pumpkin
- allspice, cinnamon, nutmeg
- large spoon
- hot plate
- large sharp knife
- pot
- bowls

Directions:

1. Carefully cut the pumpkin into halves.

2. Clean out the seeds and cut the pumpkin into long slices.

3. Carefully peel the rind from the slices.

4. Cut the slices into cubes.

5. Place the cubes and spices to taste in the pot and cover with water.

6. Bring to a boil, stirring occasionally.

7. Cook until the pumpkin is tender. Spoon into some bowls and serve warm.

Before you taste the stewed pumpkin, describe how you think it will taste.

_____

_____

After you taste the stewed pumpkin, describe how it tasted.

_____

_____

Pioneer Cookbook

Work with three or four other students to make a pioneer cookbook. Copy the following recipes for your cookbook. You may wish to include the recipes in this book for Maple Sugar Candy (page 22) and for Stewed Pumpkin (page 31). Add any other pioneer recipes that you can find. Then use posterboard to make a cover for your cookbook.

Johnnycake (cornbread)

In a large mixing bowl, combine 2 cups (0.5 L) flour, 2 cups (0.5 L) cornmeal, 6 to 8 tablespoons (90-120 mL) sugar, 2 tablespoons (30 mL) baking powder, and 1 teaspoon (5 mL) salt. In another bowl beat together 4 eggs, 2 cups (0.5 L) milk, and 1/2 cup (125 mL) melted butter. Add the egg mixture to the flour mixture and stir until it is smooth. Pour the batter into a greased 9" x 9" x 2" (23 cm x 23 cm x 5 cm) glass dish. Bake at 425°F (220°C) for 20 to 25 minutes or until golden brown. This recipe serves 18 to 20 people.

Dried Apple Pie

Place 2 cups (0.5 L) dried apples in water. Let them soak overnight. Remove the apples from the water and mix them with 1/2 cup (125 mL) sugar, 1 teaspoon (5 mL) allspice, and 1 teaspoon (5 mL) cinnamon. Pour this mixture into an 8" (20 cm) pie crust. Add 3 tablespoons (45 mL) of butter by dropping a little bit here and there in the apple mixture. Place a second crust on top and cut slit marks in it. Bake at 350°F (180°C) for about one hour or until golden brown.

Hot Cider

Pour the cider into a pot. Add a few cloves or cardamom seeds and a stick of cinnamon. Place the pot on a low heat. Do not boil.

Salt-rising Bread

In a large bowl, mix 1/2 cup (125 mL) fresh, coarse, white, water-ground cornmeal, 1 tablespoon (15 mL) sugar, and 1 tablespoon (15 mL) salt. Scald 1 cup (250 mL) milk and pour it over the cornmeal mixture. Cover and let it stand in a warm place overnight or until it ferments. (If the dough does not get light in texture, you need to start over.) In a separate bowl, combine 2 tablespoons (30 mL) sugar and 5 tablespoons (75 mL) lard. Scald 3 cups (0.75 L) milk and pour over the sugar and lard mixture. Add 3 1/2 cups (0.875 L) sifted all-purpose flour and the cornmeal mixture. Set the bowl in a pan of warm water for 1–2 hours. Be sure to replace the water when it cools so that the mixture is sitting in warm water for the entire time. Bubbles should come up from the bottom of the mixture. Add 5 cups (1.250 L) sifted all-purpose flour to the mixture. Knead and slowly add 2 1/2 cups (0.625 mL) sifted all-purpose flour into the dough until it is smooth. Put the dough in three greased 5" x 9" (13 cm x 23 cm) loaf pans. Cover and let the loaves rise until they have doubled in size. Bake at 400°F (200°C) for 10 minutes and 350°F (180°C) for 25 to 30 minutes.

You may also want to find recipes for other foods mentioned in the story, such as pumpkin pie, vinegar pie, cornmeal mush, headcheese, hickory cured ham, spareribs, butter, buttermilk, molasses candy, peppermint candy, baked beans, venison, and baked Hubbard squash.

The Boy Who Cried Wolf

You have probably heard or read the story about the shepherd who tricked the villagers into coming to his aid by crying, "Wolf!" In the story, the young shepherd was watching his family's flock of sheep in a field. It was a boring job so the boy decided he would cause some excitement. He ran from the field and yelled as loudly as he could, "Wolf! Wolf!" All of the villagers left their homes to save the boy and his flock. However, when they got to the field, they found there was no wolf, only a laughing shepherd and his flock. The shepherd had so much fun, he decided to try this trick again and again. Each time the villagers went to help him, and each time the boy only laughed at them. Then one day a wolf really appeared in the field. The shepherd really needed help! He yelled with all of his strength, "Wolf! Wolf!" But no one went to help him.

Use the Venn diagram shown below to compare *The Boy Who Cried Wolf* with what happened to Laura's Cousin Charley in Chapter 11. The parts of the circle that do not overlap show what is special about each story. The overlapping parts of the circles in the middle of the diagram show what is the same about both stories.

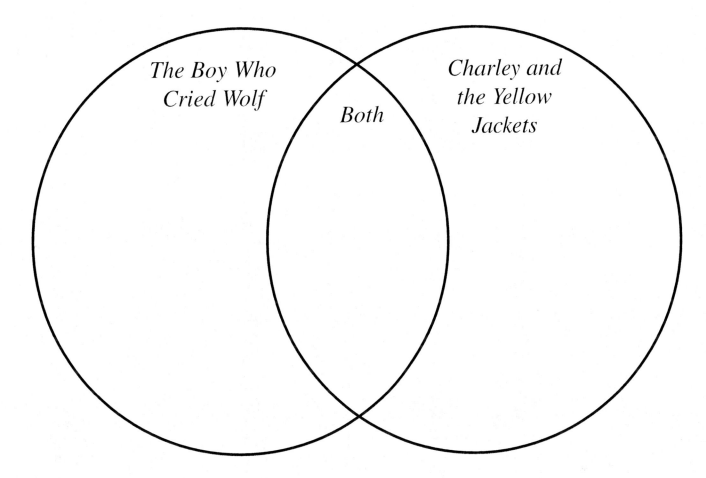

Make Your Own Autograph Book

Laura and her friends kept autograph books so they would remember each other. In the autograph books, they wrote verses and signed their names. Here is an example of something Laura's friend, Minnie Johnson, wrote to her.

When the name that I write here
Is dim on the page
And the leaves of your album
Are yellow with age,
Still think of me kindly
And do not forget
That wherever I am

I remember you yet.

　　　　–The Little House Diary by Barbara M. Walker

Make your own autograph book and have your friends sign it, just as Laura did.

Materials:

- two pieces of 5" x 8" (13 cm x 20 cm) posterboard
- ten sheets of 5" x 8" (13 cm x 20 cm) colored writing paper

Directions:

1. Decorate the cover of your autograph book.

2. Have your friends sign your book and have fun signing theirs.

3. Remember to sign in verse as Minnie did for Laura. Use the space below to write a verse that you might use to sign in someone's autograph book.

Any Questions?

When you finished reading *Little House in the Big Woods*, did you have some questions that were left unanswered? Write some of your questions here.

_____

_____

_____

Work in groups or by yourself to prepare possible answers for some or all of the questions you have asked above and those written below. When you have finished your predictions, share your ideas with the class.

- What happened to Laura's log cabin in the Big Woods?

- What is the population of Pepin, Wisconsin, today?

- Do the Big Woods still exist?

- What was school like for pioneer children?

- Why did the storekeeper admire Mary but not Laura?

- How did life change for the Ingalls after other families moved into the Big Woods?

- Why did Pa tell Mary and Laura so many stories?

- Why did Aunt Lotty tell Laura and Mary that she liked both brown and golden hair?

- Do you think that Uncle George knew that Laura was afraid of him at first?

- What happened to Uncle George in the army to make him act so "wild"?

- Who invented the first threshing machine?

- Did Charley learn anything from his experience with the yellow jackets?

- Why didn't Pa allow the girls to strike each other?

- What happened to each member of the Ingalls family?

- Did Laura live in the Big Woods when she was grown up?

- Did other pioneer families live like the Ingalls?

- Was it difficult for Ma to live in a log cabin in the woods after growing up in the East?

- Why did Laura decide to write about her childhood experiences?

- What effects did the Civil War have on the Ingalls family?

Book Report Ideas

There are many ways to do a book report. After you have finished reading *Little House in the Big Woods* choose one method of reporting that interests you. It may be a way that your teacher suggests, an idea of your own, or one of the ways below.

- **Updated Version**

  Make a chart that shows how the story events might change if they took place in modern times as opposed to the post-Civil War time period.

- **Write an Autobiography**

  Imagine that you are a child in the Ingalls family. Write an autobiography.

- **A Letter to a Character**

  In this report, you may write a letter to any character in the story. You may ask him or her any questions you wish. You may even want to offer some advice on a particular problem that arises in the story.

- **Role Playing**

  This report is one that lends itself to a group project. Work with three or four other students to dramatize a scene from the story. You may wish to use costumes and props that will help the scene come to life. After performing the scene, explain why it is an important part of the story.

- **A Mini Book**

  Using two sheets of 8.5" x 11" (22 cm x 28 cm) paper, fold into quarters and cut on the folded line, resulting in eight pages. The pages could be hole-punched and bound with colored string. The high points of the story could be summarized in sequence.

- **A Character Comes to Life!**

  Suppose one of the characters in *Little House in the Big Woods* came to life and walked into your home or school. Write about what the character sees, hears, and feels as he or she experiences the world in which you live.

- **Sales Talk**

  Dress as a salesperson. Write a sales pitch and design some kind of graphics in an effort to sell *Little House in the Big Woods* to your classmates.

- **Coming Attraction!**

  Little House in the Big Woods is about to be made into a movie, and you have been chosen to design the promotional poster. Include the title and author of the book, a listing of the main characters and the contemporary actors who will play them, an illustration of a scene from the book, and a brief synopsis of the story.

- **Make a Photo Album**

  Draw a series of pictures to represent photographs showing important events in the story. Then make an album for your pictures.

Research Ideas

Describe three things that you read in *Little House in the Big Woods* that you would like to learn more about.

1. _____

2. _____

3. _____

As you read *Little House in the Big Woods*, you encountered true-life people and events, pioneer customs and celebrations, delicious foods, and the lifestyle of pioneer farmers. To increase your understanding of the characters and events of the book, as well as appreciate Laura Ingalls Wilder's craft as a writer, research to find out more about these people, places, and things.

Work in groups to research one or more of the areas you named above or the areas that are listed below. Share your findings with the rest of the class in any appropriate format for oral presentation.

- Pepin, Wisconsin
- venison
- herbal medicine
- smoking meat
- early machines
- braiding straw hats
- quilting
- square dancing
- churning butter
- types of knives
- pioneers
  - education
  - home life
  - families
  - clothing
  - folklore
  - recipes
  - music
  - celebrations

- animals
  - brindle bulldogs
  - wolves
  - bears
  - foxes
  - deer
  - panthers
  - muskrats
  - mink
  - otters
  - squirrels
  - cottontail rabbits
  - field mice
  - snowbirds
  - yellow jackets
- plants
  - leafing hazel bushes
  - buttercups

- violets
- thimble flowers
- starry grassflowers
- oak trees
- maple trees
- walnuts
- hickory nuts
- hazelnuts
- corn
  - origin
  - different types
  - growing seasons
  - recipes
- the Ingalls family
- Laura Ingalls Wilder

Presenting the Story

Have students pick one or more of the following ideas to present the book using pictures. Have them work on these activities in cooperative learning groups. Display their finished products on a wall or bulletin board or in a learning center. Be sure to display them for your Laura Ingalls Celebration, as described on pages 39–40.

- ### Quilted Story

  Adapt the directions on page 26 for this activity. Cut nine squares from white construction paper for a patchwork quilt. Ask students to use the squares to illustrate nine events from the story. After students have finished making the illustrations, have them arrange the squares in order according to the events in the story. Glue the illustrations in the correct order to the quilt.

- ### Big Book

  Have students make a big book that tells the story. Punch three holes on the left-hand side of six pieces of posterboard. Have students use one piece of posterboard to create a cover for their big book. Then have them use the rest of the posterboard to illustrate five events from the story and write a short summary of each event. Ask students to put the pieces of posterboard in order according to the events in the story. After the pieces of posterboard are in order, have students connect the pages with metal rings or yarn. Allow students to use their big book to retell the story to younger children.

- ### Bulletin Board Book

  Have students make a bulletin board book that tells the story. Divide a bulletin board in half. Use one side of the bulletin board to display the title and credits. Have students write the title and credits on a shape that reflects something that is important to the story. Then ask them to use five large sheets of butcher paper to illustrate five events from the story. You may wish to have them write a short summary of each event. Arrange the illustrations in the order of events in the story. Then staple the tops of the pages to the bulletin board. Students should be able to flip up the pages to look at each page of the bulletin board book.

- ### Multimedia Presentation

  Have students use posterboard to illustrate events from the story. Have them practice retelling the events that go with the illustrations. Ask students to add sound effects to their story. Some examples of sound effects are stomping feet, clapping hands, rubbing a wooden spoon on the face of a grater, tapping glasses filled with different amounts of water in them, and blowing in an empty raisin box to make a bugle sound. Have students record their sound effects on cassette tape. Then have them retell the story events to the class while showing their illustrations and incorporating their sound effects. Videotape the presentations so students can evaluate themselves.

Host a Laura Ingalls Celebration

Divide the class into cooperative learning groups and have a Laura Ingalls Celebration. You may wish to invite other classes to participate in this event. Use some of the activities suggested on pages 39 and 40, or have students brainstorm or do research to make lists of their own.

Here are some things your students can do to prepare for this event.

1. Have students design a variety of murals that show events in the story. Display the murals in the classroom or in the hallway.

2. Have students make a model of a covered wagon.

3. Have students use butcher paper or cloth to make clothes like the pioneers wore. Ask students to use the illustrations in the book, or do research to see what kind of clothing was popular in the 1860's. Some possible suggestions are bow ties, kerchiefs, chaps, aprons, long dresses, knickers, top hats, and coonskin caps.

4. Have students display the things they made doing the activities in this unit, such as the patchwork quilts.

5. Have students make invitations to ask other classes to come to this special event. Have them make advertisements to display in the hallway that will make teachers and students want to attend.

6. Have students make an old-time newspaper describing the events that will be taking place at the Laura Ingalls Celebration.

7. Have students write letters to the following address to purchase actual photographs from the Ingalls family.

Almanzo and Laura Ingalls Wilder Association
P.O. Box 283
Malone, NY 12953

Suggested Activities for Centers at the Laura Ingalls Celebration

Dipping Candles: Using kitchen safety rules, help students melt two bars of paraffin in a double boiler. Use a low heat and be sure the bottom part of the boiler has plenty of water. If the wax gets too hot and catches on fire, throw baking soda on it. Let the wax cool a little. Tie a cotton string to a stick. Dip the string into the paraffin. Let the wax cool a bit, then dip it again.

Role Playing: Have students dramatize scenes from the story.

Stuffed Animals: Display a list of the animals named in the story. Then have them make stuffed animals using wrapping paper. Have them fold the wrapping paper in half and draw the animals. When they cut along the lines they have drawn, they should have two shapes that are the same. Next, have students glue the shapes together three-quarters of the way along the outside edge. Then have them use tissue paper to stuff the animals. Finally, have students finish gluing the two shapes together.

Pioneer Cooking: Have students make some of the recipes that they included in their pioneer cookbooks on page 32.

Host a Laura Ingalls Celebration *(cont.)*

Making a Popsicle Loom: Have students use twelve popsicle sticks to make a loom. Tape eight of the sticks together after placing them one on top of the other. Drill a hole that is 1/8" (.32 cm) in diameter in the stack of sticks. Glue the ends of the sticks with the holes onto two sticks without holes so that they look like a railroad track with tiny holes up the middle. Glue the last two sticks on top of the sticks with holes in them. (The ends of the sticks with holes in them should be between the sticks without holes in them.) Weave yarn over and under the popsicle sticks.

Autograph Signing: Invite your guests to sign students' autograph books using verses as described on page 34.

Snowflakes: Have students make snowflakes by gluing three popsicle sticks together so they criss-cross. Allow the glue to dry. Glue styrofoam popcorn along one side of the sticks. Place drops of glue on the styrofoam and then sprinkle with silver glitter. Allow the glue to dry.

Story Time: Have students take turns sitting in a rocking chair and reading aloud their favorite parts of the story. Or they may wish to read aloud other stories about pioneer life.

Making a Log Cabin: Have students cut 14 twigs so they are all the same length. Put two twigs on the table. At opposite ends have them glue two more twigs so that they overlap the first two twigs. Let the glue dry. Then add two more twigs that overlap the second pair of twigs. Continue gluing two twigs at a time and then letting them dry. Ask them to use colored construction paper or posterboard for the roof of the cabin. Have students glue the roof onto the twigs.

Making a Cradle: Have students use boxes and posterboard to make a cradle.

Photo in a Nut: Have students draw pictures the size of a walnut shell of the characters in the story. Have them spread glue over the flat edge of half a walnut shell. Then have them place the picture flat on the glue.

Being a Tinsmith: Have students use aluminum foil and pretend that it is tin. They can use a variety of objects to make impressions in the tin. In addition, they can use something like a popsicle stick to draw different designs.

Herbal Medicine Ads: Have students make advertisements for herbal medicines.

Dolls: Have students use material scraps to make a rag doll, or a corncob to make a corncob doll.

Unit Test

Matching: Write the letters to match the descriptions with the characters' names.

1. _____ Pa
2. _____ Ma
3. _____ Mary
4. _____ Charley
5. _____ Grandpa
6. _____ Uncle George
7. _____ Laura
8. _____ Sukey
9. _____ Carrie
10. _____ Jack

A. A well-behaved girl who always obeys

B. A gentle man, who plays the fiddle

C. A brown-haired girl who loves to be outside

D. A kind woman and a wonderful cook

E. A brindle bulldog and a wonderful watchdog

F. The naughty cousin stung by yellow jackets

G. The maple syrup expert who hosted a dance

H. The gentle brown cow

I. The wild bugle player home from the army

J. Laura's younger sister

True or False: Answer true or false next to each statement.

1. _____ Cousin Charley is a well behaved, wonderful boy.

2. _____ Laura thinks that Mary's hair is prettier than hers.

3. _____ Laura loved sitting still on Sundays.

4. _____ Pa's "Bear in the Way" was really a tree stump.

5. _____ Uncle George danced with Laura at Grandpa's house.

Essay: Answer this essay question on the back of this paper.

Laura and Mary lived a life very different from our lives today. Write an essay that describes their lives, tells how they lived differently than you do, and tell if you would rather live as Laura did, or as you do today. Tell why you feel as you do.

Response

Explain the meaning of each of these quotations from *Little House in the Big Woods*.

Chapter 1:   *A wagon track ran before the house, turning and twisting out of sight in the woods where the wild animals lived, but the little girl did not know where it went, nor what might be at the end of it.*

Chapter 1:   *Her father would say, 'Go to sleep, Laura. Jack won't let the wolves in.'*

Chapter 2:   *When Pa came back he had both a bear and a pig in the wagon.*

Chapter 2:   *'Well!' he said to her. 'You're only a little half-pint of cider half drunk up, but by Jinks! you're as strong as a little French horse!'*

Chapter 3:   *He said, 'If you'd obeyed me, as you should, you wouldn't have been out in the Big Woods after dark, and you wouldn't have been scared by a screech-owl.'*

Chapter 4:   *She was so beautiful that Laura could not say a word. She just held her tight and forgot everything else.*

Chapter 5:   *The sled went right under the hog and picked him up. With a squeal he sat down on James, and he kept on squealing, long and loud and shrill . . .*

Chapter 6:   *Just then one of the dancing little bits of light from the lantern jumped between the bars of the gate, and Laura saw long, shaggy, black fur, and two little, glittering eyes.*

Chapter 7:   *'Why is it sugar snow, Pa?' she asked him, . . .*

Chapter 8:   *Laura could not keep her feet still. Uncle George looked at her and laughed. Then he caught her by the hand and did a little dance with her, in the corner.*

Chapter 9:   *The storekeeper said to Pa and Ma, 'That's a pretty little girl you've got there,' and he admired Mary's golden curls. But he did not say anything about Laura, or about her curls.*

Chapter 9:   *She did not mind very much when Pa laughed at her for being such a greedy little girl that she took more than she could carry away.*

Chapter 10:   *Pa's blue eyes shone down at her, and he said, 'Well, Laura, my hair is brown.'*

Chapter 11:   *But she didn't understand why Pa had called him a little liar. She didn't understand how Charley could be a liar, when he had not said a word.*

Chapter 12:   *Autumn was great fun. There was so much work to do, so many good things to eat, so many new things to see.*

Chapter 13:   *She was glad that the cozy house, and Pa and Ma and the firelight and the music, were now. They could not be forgotten, she thought, because now is now. It can never be a long time ago.*

Note to the Teacher: Choose an appropriate number of quotes for your students.

Conversations

Work in groups to write and perform the conversations that might have occurred in each of the following situations.

- Laura and Ma watch the fire as the venison cooks. *(2 persons)*

- Laura and Mary play house in the attic with their dolls. *(2 persons)*

- Pa tells Laura and Mary a story as he greases his traps. *(3 persons)*

- Laura and Mary help Ma with the chores. *(3 persons)*

- Pa plays "Mad Dog" with Laura and Mary. *(3 persons)*

- Pa tells Mary and Laura the story about Grandpa and the panther. *(3 persons)*

- Laura and Mary play in the snow with their cousins, Alice, Ella, and Peter. *(5 persons)*

- Laura celebrates Christmas with her doll, Charlotte. *(2 persons)*

- Pa tells his story about Grandpa's sled and the pig. *(3 persons)*

- Laura and Ma talk after Ma accidentally slaps the bear on the shoulder. *(2 persons)*

- Laura and her cousin, Laura, argue about which baby is prettiest. *(2 persons)*

- Uncle George and Laura dance. *(2 persons)*

- The storekeeper talks to Laura and her family. *(6 persons)*

- Ma, Pa, Laura, Mary, and Baby Carrie have a picnic at Lake Pepin. *(5 persons)*

- Laura and Pa talk after Laura slaps Mary. *(2 persons)*

- Pa and Uncle Henry harvest the grain. *(2 persons)*

- Pa and Ma talk to Laura and Mary about Cousin Charley and the yellow jackets. *(4 persons)*

- Laura helps Ma make pumpkin pie. *(2 persons)*

- Ma, Pa, Laura, Mary, and Baby Carrie are all snug and cozy by the fire. *(5 persons)*

Bibliography of Related Reading

Books for Students

Anderson, William. *Laura Ingalls Wilder, Pioneer and Author.* (Kipling Press, 1987)

Blair, Gwenda. *Laura Ingalls Wilder.* (Putnam Publishing Group, 1981)

Giff, Patricia Reilly. *Laura Ingalls Wilder: Growing Up in the Little House.* (Puffin Books, 1987)

Gunby, Lise. *Early Farm Life.* (Crabtree Publishing Company, 1983)

Hamilton, Dorothy. *Daniel Forbes: A Pioneer Boy.* (Barnwood Press, 1980)

Lane, Rose Wilder. *Let the Hurricane Roar.* (Harper & Row, 1933)

Naden, C.J. *I Can Read About Pioneers.* (Troll Associates, 1979)

Sabin, Francene. *Pioneers.* (Troll Associates, 1985)

Shaw, Janet. *Kirsten Learns a Lesson: A School Story.* (Pleasant Company, 1990)

Walker, Barbara M. *The Little House Diary.* (Madison Press, 1979)

Wilder, Laura Ingalls. *Farmer Boy.* (Harper & Row, 1953)

Wilder, Laura Ingalls. *Little House on the Prairie.* (Harper & Row, 1953)

Wilder, Laura Ingalls. *On the Banks of Plum Creek.* (Harper & Row, 1953)

Wilder, Laura Ingalls. *Women of Our Time Series.* (Puffin Books, 1988)

References and Teacher Resources

Anderson, William. *The Plum Creek Story of Laura Ingalls Wilder.* (Anderson, 1987)

Anderson, William and Kelly, Leslie. *Little House Country: A Photo Guide to the Homesites of Laura Ingalls Wilder.* (Anderson, 1989)

Anderson, William T. *Laura Ingalls Wilder Country.* (HarperCollins, 1990)

Anderson, William T. *Laura Ingalls Wilder Country: The People & Places in Laura Ingalls Wilder's Life & Books.* (HarperCollins, 1990)

Artman, John. *Pioneers.* (Good Apple, 1987)

Calhoun, Sharon C. and English, Billy J. *The Wisconsin Story.* (Apple Corps Publications, 1987)

Kalman, Bobbie. *Early Settler Life Series.* (Crabtree Publishing Company, 1982)

Wilder, Laura Ingalls. *West from Home: Letters of Laura Ingalls Wilder, San Francisco 1915.* (HarperCollins, 1976)

Zochert, Donald. *Laura: The Life of Laura Ingalls Wilder.* (Avon, 1977)

Cookbooks and Activities

Garson, Eugenia. *The Laura Ingalls Wilder Songbook.* (Harper, 1968)

Stenson, Elizabeth. *Early Settler Activity Guide.* (Crabtree Publishing Company, 1988)

Walker, Barbara. *The Little House Cookbook.* (Harper & Row, 1979)

Answer Key

Page 10

1. Accept appropriate responses.
2. Laura Ingalls Wilder is the author.
3. The setting of the story is the Big Woods of Wisconsin in the late 1860's.
4. Mary and Laura liked the pig's tail the best. They liked it best because it was fun to cook, it smelled good as it cooked, and it tasted delicious.
5. A trundle bed is a small bed that slides under a larger bed.
6. Laura's doll, Susan, was a corncob doll.
7. Pa shot the bear, and the bear had the pig in its arms.
8. Grandpa was coming home through the Big Woods, and a hungry panther chased him. Grandpa didn't have his gun with him. He barely made it home, grabbed his gun, and shot the panther.
9. In the game "Mad Dog," Pa messed up his hair, got down on his hands and knees, growled, and chased the girls until they were cornered. Answers will vary as to why the girls enjoyed playing the game.
10. Answers will vary.

Page 12

Possible answers include:

Panthers

I. Description
   A. Large cat that is all black
   B. Length with tail — about 120 inches (300 centimeters)
   C. Weight –110 – 200 pounds (50 – 90 kilograms)
II. Habitat
   A. Most commonly found in the Far East
   B. Also found in Central Asia, Asia Minor, and Africa

III. Foods
   A. Carnivore — meat eater
   B. Food sources — antelope, young cattle, pigs, other animals.

Page 13

Page 14

The description of Laura's home may include the following: sturdy log cabin; surrounded by woods and wild animals; no neighbors; a wagon track in front of the house; upstairs, a large attic; downstairs, small bedroom that had a window with a wooden shutter and the big room that had a front and back door and two glass windows; crooked rail fence surrounded the house; and two large oak trees in front of the house.

Answer Key *(cont.)*

Page 15

1. Accept appropriate answers.

2. A screech owl was the "voice in the woods."

3. Laura and Mary made molasses candy by carefully pouring a boiling mixture of molasses and sugar into pans of snow. The snow made the molasses mixture harden.

4. Aunt Eliza, Uncle Peter, Peter, Alice, and Ella came to visit Laura's family.

5. Laura, Mary, and their cousins played outdoors and made pictures by falling off of a stump into the snow.

6. There was a panther at the spring and Prince wanted to protect Aunt Eliza.

7. Laura received red mittens, peppermint candy, and a rag doll which she named Charlotte.

8. Every Sunday, Laura and Mary put on their best clothes and sat quietly while Ma read stories from the *Bible* or Pa read them stories from *The Wonders of the Animal World*.

9. Suggested answer: Grandpa and his brothers did not like sitting still on Sunday. When their father fell asleep, they went quietly outside. They got on their sled and went sliding down a hill when they ran into a pig. They couldn't stop, so the pig went for a ride, too. At the end of the day, Grandpa's father spanked him and his brothers because they hadn't honored the Sabbath.

10. Laura received a little wooden man, five little cakes, and a new dress for Charlotte. Pa also played the fiddle for her.

Page 20

1. Accept appropriate answers.

2. Ma and Laura thought that it was Sukey in the pen, but it was really a very large bear.

3. Pa brought them candy and calico for new dresses.

4. It was really an old tree stump.

5. *Sugar snow* means that it snows late in the year making a longer run of sap so more maple sugar can be made.

6. Grandpa made maple syrup from the sap.

7. Pa and Grandpa carried the hot maple syrup with wooden yokes that fit over their shoulders. On each side of a yoke there was a wooden bucket hanging at the end of a chain and a hook.

8. Answers will vary. Answers may include the following: wore a blue army coat with brass buttons; bold; merry blue eyes; big and broad; walked with a swagger; wild; played the bugle; and joked, laughed, and danced.

9. Laura and her cousin, Laura, argued over which baby was prettier.

10. Answers will vary. Descriptions may include the following: George blew his bugle; Pa played his fiddle; skirts swirled; boots stamped; circles went round and round; everyone was laughing; everybody clapped to the music; everybody was excited; and George and Grandma had a jigging contest.

Answer Key *(cont.)*

Page 25

1. Accept appropriate responses.
2. They were under two big oak trees. There was soft green grass on the ground. Green leaves were the roofs.
3. Pa would wait until fall when the fawn could live without its mother.
4. At the edge of the lake, there was a large gray building made of boards. There was sand spread all around the building. This was the store. Behind the store there was a large clearing. There were a lot of smaller buildings that were houses. Some of the houses were yellow because they were made from newly-cut boards. Other houses were gray because they were made from older boards. There were more houses than Laura could count.
5. The storekeeper gave each girl a piece of candy. Mary's candy had a poem on it. Laura's candy just had one line on it.
6. The weight of the pebbles tore Laura's pocket, causing them to fall into the wagon.
7. Laura thought Clarence was more fun than Eva. Eva played carefully and kept her dress clean, but Clarence laughed, ran, shouted, and climbed trees.
8. Laura had worried that Aunt Lotty would like Mary's hair best.
9. Pa spanked Laura because she slapped Mary in the face.
10. Pa got the honey away from the bear by waving a huge club and yelling to scare it away and by cutting the tree down and sawing it in half so the bees would leave.

Page 28

Suggested answers:

The queen bee lays the eggs so more bees are born.

The workers gather food and take care of the young bees.

The drones mate with the queen.

The workers make the hive using special glands that make beeswax. They chew the wax to make six-sided cells. Some cells will store the queen's eggs. Other cells will store pollen so the nectar from flowers can be changed into honey.

At the flower, a worker honey bee uses its long tongue to suck nectar out of a flower. The nectar is stored in the bee's honey stomach.

The worker who found the flowers tells the other workers where the flowers are by doing a dance when it returns to the hive. If the flowers are less than 100 yards away, the bee dances in circles, first to the right then to the left. If the flowers are more than 100 yards away, the bee dances a pattern that looks like a figure-8.

Page 30

1. Accept appropriate answers.
2. A cradle is a sharp steel blade attached to a frame of wooden slats. It has a long curved handle.
3. The grain had to be put in the shock before dark because it would spoil if it got wet from dew or rain.
4. Possible answers include: big boy, almost 11 years old; could jump from stump to stump; spoiled; made trouble whenever he could; and naughty.
5. Ma and Aunt Polly covered him with mud, wrapped him in an old sheet, and gave him herbs for the fever.

Answer Key *(cont.)*

Page 30 *(cont.)*

6. Charley had lied by pretending that there was something wrong with him when there wasn't.
7. Ma braided the straw to make hats.
8. The "wonderful machine" was used for threshing.
9. Eight horsepower means it takes eight horses to make it go.
10. Answers will vary.

Page 33

The Boy Who Cried Wolf
shepherd
watching sheep in a field
yelled there was a wolf
villagers came to help
eaten by the wolf
Charley and the Yellow Jackets
Laura's cousin
was out in the field with Pa and Uncle Henry
kept getting in the way
was told to go away
just yelled
Pa and Uncle Henry came to help
stung by yellow jackets
Both
were bored
yelled for help
people came running to help
laughed at the joke they played on others
played the joke on others several times
when help was really needed, no one came

Pages 38–40

Create a display of these culminating activities for the bulletin board, shelf, or learning center.

Page 41

Matching

1. B
2. D
3. A
4. F
5. G
6. I
7. C
8. H
9. J
10. E

True or False

1. False
2. True
3. False
4. True
5. True

Essay

Accept appropriate answers.

Page 42

Accept all reasonable and well-supported answers.

Page 43

Perform the conversations in class. Ask students to respond to the conversations in several different ways, such as, "Are the conversations realistic?" or, "Are the words the characters say in line with their personalities?"